Great Locofoco Juggernaut

Great Locofoco Juggernaut,

A NEW Console-a-tory Sub-Treasury

RAG-MONSTER:

A Cartoon Bank Note by

D. C. JOHNSTON

―――――

By Malcolm Johnson

IMPRINT SOCIETY

BARRE, MASSACHUSETTS

1971

ACKNOWLEDGMENTS

MY THANKS *go to David Tatham, Draper Hill, Sinclair Hitchings, and the staff of the American Antiquarian Society, who have so continuously assisted me in these efforts with their generosity in both time and knowledge. And my thanks also go to Barbara Pike for her patience, comments, and efforts in typing the manuscript.*

Especially I want to express my continued indebtedness to my good friends, Mr. and Mrs. E. F. Freeman, D. C. Johnston's great-grandson and his wife, who have so greatly stimulated my interest in their illustrious ancestor.

M. J.

CONTENTS

D. C. Johnston: A Biographical Sketch.

DAVID CLAYPOOL JOHNSTON was born in Philadelphia on March 25, 1798. The son of William P. and Charlotte Rowson Johnston, David was named for his father's former employer David Claypool, Philadelphia printer and publisher of the *Pennsylvania Packet* and *Claypool's Daily American Advertiser.*

Little is known currently of Johnston's early years. If, however, the autobiographical sketch he produced for William Dunlap in 1833 may be believed, he was a bright but lazy student. Showing little interest in matters academic, he appears to have expended much effort caricaturing those around him, to the pleasure of his fellows and the wrath of his instructors.

> In figures (that is, caricature figures), I was more successful; these I usually exchanged with some of my fellow scholars, for a slate full of such figures as suited the preceptor, who not unfrequently approved of my calculations, without calculating himself, that they were received as a quid pro quo, for a wretched attempt at a likeness of himself or his assistants.[1]

Leaving school some eighteen months before completing his studies, Johnston became apprenticed to Francis Kearney, a Philadelphia engraver. Though he would have preferred a career in painting, such a course was viewed as impractical. His first attempts at the techniques of etching and engraving

---

1. William Dunlap, *History of the Rise and Progress of the Arts of Design in the United States*, p. 113.

were produced March 12 and 15, 1815.[2] During the following four years, he undoubtedly produced numerous illustrations over a Kearney imprint. Only a few are known,
however, and these only by lucky circumstance. A scrapbook
exists which, while somewhat picked over, includes not only
engravings collected by Johnston but also a series of proof
illustrations for a collection of Shakespeare's plays, all bearing the imprint Tanner, Vallence, Kearney & Co. Sc. These
were produced for an edition by Durrell, New York, 1817-
18. Six of the proofs bear the pencilled signature *D. C. Johnston Sc(ulpsi)t.*

Completing his apprenticeship in 1819, Johnston struck
out on his own. Business was bad, however, and he found
himself reduced to engraving nameplates and dog collars.
He did illustrate at least one book, *Ephemera or the History
of Cockney Dandies*, containing four engravings which he
signed "Gibolibus Crackfardi FRSA LLD." In addition,
two single sheet caricature engravings exist which were
most likely executed during that first year, "A Militia Mus-
ter" and "A Splendid Procession of Freemasons."

Not finding enough work in the depression of 1819, Johnston turned to the stage, making his debut as Henry in
Speed the Plough at The New Theatre in Philadelphia.
Though his initial performance was not by his own admis-
sion superb, his competence increased sufficiently to the
point that he played opposite the celebrated English actor
Charles Mathews during the latter's American trip in 1822-23.

Johnston continued his artistic efforts during these years,
engraving, among other things, the first of his famous comic

---

2. These two small engravings may be found in the American Antiquarian
Society, Worcester, Mass. They are mounted on a sheet of paper bearing the
inscription, "The first productions of David C. Johnston commencing March
of 1815."

theatrical portraits showing Mr. Mathews in various roles. That he painted as well there can be little doubt, though few works from his Philadelphia days exist aside from several wash drawings.

He moved to Boston in 1825 in time for the theatre season. There he continued his etching and engraving, developing numerous contacts with local artists and authors who might need the talents of an illustrator. Though he remained on the stage, he received mixed reviews and when he secured enough commissions he "cut the boards" to "cut copper."[3]

His association with the theatre prompted him to continue the comic actor portraits during the twenties with a series of etchings, engravings, and later lithographs. Many well known actors and actresses were so portrayed in their best roles. Some twenty-five of these theatrical portraits are known.

In 1825 Johnston, along with other Boston artists, was chosen by John Pendleton, lately returned from France, to try his hand at the new graphic technique of lithography. For these attempts Pendleton furnished stone and crayon which he had acquired while abroad.[4] The first published piece depicting an old mill, which appeared in the *Boston Monthly Magazine* for December 1825, was by Johnston. This was the beginning of a long and fruitful career with the Pendletons. These efforts included the first dated lithographed sheet music cover, *The Log House*, March 14, 1826, and numerous social and political satires, and theatrical portraits.

Publishing was by no means new to Johnston. However, in 1828 he began on a larger scale with the first volume of *Scraps*, an oblong quarto in paper covers. Each volume con-

3. Dunlap, p. 116.
4. *Boston Monthly Magazine*, Vol. I, No. VII, December 1825, p. 384.

tained four copper plate etchings, each of which consisted of nine to twelve or more separate caricature vignettes. Numbers Two to Eight were published between 1830 and 1840, and Number One, Second Series, was produced in 1849. Designed after Cruikshank's *Scraps and Sketches*, first published in 1827, these bits of whimsy delighted many readers. Covering all manner of human activity and attitudes of the day, these *Scraps* were always well received. Their popularity earned for Johnston first the soubriquet the "American Hogarth" and later, by 1835, the "American Cruikshank."[5] In 1828, Johnston contributed a comic watercolor, "The Muses," to the first exhibition held at the new Boston Athenaeum.

As if his lithographs, book illustrations, and publications were not enough to keep him busy, Johnston was also actively courting the lovely Sarah Murphy of Concord. He was to marry Sarah in 1830 when she was in her twentieth year.

The period of Johnston's greatest efforts began soon after he arrived in Boston. Self-taught in painting and lithography, he was by then proficient in every medium available to him at the time. Though lacking the maturity exemplified in his later work, there was no question of his abilities. Intelligent, well versed in the work of both classic and current authors, he often quoted Shakespeare, Milton, Cowper, and Swift to add further satire to a particular subject. He also produced occasional poems or a bit of prose himself.

Some of his best known pieces were produced during these earlier years coincident with the beginnings of Jacksonian Democracy. Few political figures of the nineteenth century were satirized as much as Andrew Jackson. Certainly Jackson

---

5. *New York Transcript*, January 6, 1835.

was one of Johnston's favorite targets; no one individual was to occupy him so thoroughly and with such regularity throughout his career.

Beginning in 1824 Johnston caricatured Jackson in "A Foot-Race" showing Jackson, Adams, Crawford, and Clay racing for the presidency. In 1828 he launched a far more devastating and much more sophisticated attack against Old Hickory than the "Coffin Handbill" had been; also referring to Jackson's treatment of the Militia deserters in 1817, this cartoon portrays Jackson as "Richard III," the lineaments of his face made up of the bodies of slain soldiers. Below is the quotation from Shakespeare, "Methought the souls of all that I had murder'd came to my tent." (*Richard III*, Act 5, Sc. 3).

Further satires produced by Johnston about Jackson include "Symptoms of a Locked Jaw," "Race over Uncle Sam's Course 4th March 1833," "Exhibition of Cabinet Pictures," "Illustration of the adventures and achievements of the renowned Don Quixote & his doughty squire Sancho Panza," "Illustrations of Phrenology," and "Annexation, Or sport for grown Children." These represent a few of Johnston's single sheet satirical endeavors. Others undoubtedly exist; however, Johnston did not always sign his works and identification can sometimes be difficult.[6]

In addition to the aforesaid, Johnston designed the comical bank note here under discussion. It is especially interesting to note that he designed genuine bank notes and stock certificates. Proofs of notes for two banks and one stock certificate have been located in his personal effects. The certificate is signed, but the notes are not. The first of these

---

6. Johnston also used a number of pseudonyms: Fun, Whigsby, Seatsfield, Snooks, Nobody, Corkscrew, Tintoretto Mavrikadart, and the aforementioned Gebolibus Crackfardi.

are $100 and $500 denomination notes on the Ohio Exporting and Importing Company, Cincinnati, bearing the imprint Tanner Kearney & Tiebout and most likely engraved while Johnston was an apprentice. The others are struck from a single plate and are $1, $2, $3, and $5 denominations for the Oriental Bank of Boston, circa 1835, and bear the imprint of the New England Banknote Co., Boston. It is extremely likely that Johnston engraved others, particularly for the latter firm. However, until manuscript material or company records come to light, it is almost impossible to determine which they might be.

Though Johnston continued producing single sheet caricatures and book illustrations, his output by the mid-1840s had decreased considerably as he turned more to the teaching of art. He also established two of the earliest commercial art programs in America. In part this change may be attributed to the arrival of newer and cheaper processes of reproduction in the graphic arts, particularly in book illustration. It would

appear, however, on the evidence of known surviving examples, that he continued painting and produced an occasional political cartoon. Certainly he continued his contri-
butions to the Boston Athenaeum exhibitions until 1861.[7]
His last engraving was published in 1863.

David Claypool Johnston died in November of 1865 after
a long illness at his home in Dorchester. News clippings
show that he was much respected as a citizen and teacher.
His career as a social and political satirist seems by then to
have been forgotten.

7. Malcolm Johnson, *David Claypool Johnston, American Graphic Humorist,
1789-1865*, p. 16.

A Short History of the Events Leading to
the Founding of the Sub-Treasury.

Andrew Jackson's term of office was certainly contro-
versial and the issue of the U. S. Bank was only one of many
which plagued him. South Carolina attempted nullification
of the Constitution; there was the Indian question; expansion
westward was well advanced; and though carefully avoided
as a political issue, slavery as an institution was becoming
questioned more and more.

Though the caricature discussed here was not issued until
late 1837, well after Van Buren's election, it had its ante-
cedents during Jackson's Presidency. Indeed, the Bank question predates Old Hickory.

In order to appreciate the Locofoco bank note, it is necessary to review briefly the very complex series of events leading up to what is referred to as the Bank War and the subsequent founding of the sub-treasury.

The Bank of the United States, brain child of Alexander
Hamilton, was founded early in 1791. Modeled closely on
the Bank of England, with the right to establish branches in
different parts of the country, the BUS was to be a repository
of federal funds to be administered principally by private
interest. It was also designed as a mechanism through which
these government deposits could stabilize the economy by
maintaining a standard value on government securities.
Should the securities drop below par, the Bank could buy
them back, thereby raising their value. With a sound economic system, the United States could then pay off both
foreign and domestic debts, many of which had been in-
curred during the Revolution. By August of 1791, United

States 6 percent securities were selling above par in London and Amsterdam. By 1795 the foreign debt was paid. (It was 1835 before the domestic debt was paid.) The Bank, so far successful in its purpose, was rechartered in 1816 for an additional twenty years.

After the War of 1812, with the usual postwar optimism and overextension of credit, inflation developed, culminating in panic and depression in 1819. Indulging in speculation themselves, the directors of the BUS waited too long to curb these activities. It was not until late 1818 that steps were taken. Branches were allowed to accept no bills but their own; they were to present for payment all drafts on state banks, and they could renew no personal loans or mortgages. But by then it was too late; in fact, these measures when implemented only hastened the panic. The West was hardest hit, as specie flowed east, leaving in its wake bankruptcy and a large debtor population. Furthermore, the South and West were dependent on the land, and southern planters became concerned over decreasing profits as the period saw the industrialization of the northern and middle states with the capitalist organization of what had formerly been journeyman industries. Discontent spread. Whether from loss of ownership over means of production, separation from direct contacts with markets, increased feelings of social and economic inequality with their moneyed fellows, or from the strain of new discipline, stirrings and mutterings began among working men which would influence the next decades.

By 1820 the crisis which had begun to die down in the East was worsening in the West. Outbursts were provoked by Bank tactics, the most spectacular of which was the Relief War in Kentucky. Under pressure many states passed "relief" legislation in the form of stop laws, stays of execution, and the establishment of state banks empowered to issue millions in paper currency. This, of course, created additional inflation rather than relief. The situation was such that creditors were seen running from debtors, the latter anxious to pay off their obligations in the worthless paper currency.[8]

Andrew Jackson had weathered the panic of 1819 fairly well and prospects for the future were bright. At this time Jackson was serving as governor of the Territory of Florida. On October 5, 1821, he resigned that position and prepared to leave for home. While President Monroe's request to reconsider was still in the mail, Jackson returned to the Hermitage and his wife Rachel. There he began to undertake the job of making himself comfortable in his retirement from public office. Luckily, his cotton crop of 1821 was good and he looked forward to a life as planter, husband, and father of several adopted children then in school. His retirement was short-lived.

As early as 1822, overtures were made to Jackson concerning the possibility of his candidacy for the presidential election of 1824. At every attempt he repeated his desire to remain in retirement. By April of 1822, however, a group of Jackson's friends and supporters known as the "Nashville Junto" had determined his fate. Over the next year further assistance was gained and plans were laid. The first of these was implemented on October 1, 1823, when Old Hickory was elected United States senator by the Tennessee Legislature, clutching triumph from the heretofore favored candidate John Williams.[9] Reluctantly, Jackson left his beloved Rachel for Washington. Although his term of office was not particularly distinguished, he was a conscientious worker and seldom absent when the Senate was in session.

8. W. M. Gouge, *A Short History of Paper Money and Banking in the United States*, Part ii, p. 234.

9. Marquis James, *The Wife of Andrew Jackson*, p. 61.

The campaign of 1824 was a quiet one. All four candidates —Henry Clay, John Quincy Adams, William H. Crawford, and Andrew Jackson—shared similar views on all major issues. No one campaigned extensively and the newspapers were decent. And no one attained a majority in the electoral college. Jackson was first, Adams second, Crawford third, and Clay a decided last. By offering Clay the office of secretary of state, Adams men were able to gain Clay's electoral support. Overtures were made to Jackson by Clay supporters for a similar deal but he would not buy. In February 1825 when the decision went to the House of Representatives, Adams was elected on the first ballot by a majority of one state. Clay was subsequently offered the number one cabinet post. Victory was legitimate but hollow. Jackson resigned his Senate seat and returned to Tennessee. But this was not meant to be retirement. The cry "we was robbed" was raised by Jackson supporters and electioneering began for the campaign of 1828.

The campaign of 1828, which had begun before Adams' inauguration in 1825, was the first mudslinging presidential contest. Jackson men were accusing Adams of purchasing "gaming tables and gambling furniture" out of public funds, in reality a billiards table and chess set which Adams paid for himself.[10] The Adams press was not inactive. The famous "Coffin Handbill" was produced, alluding to Jackson's execution of insubordinate militiamen in the Florida campaign in 1817; Rachel Jackson's virtue was questioned; and, of course, much was made of Jackson's frontier brawling. In all, it was the most degrading campaign thus far in history.

The Jackson-Calhoun and Adams-Clay factions of 1823-28 represented the beginnings of the Democratic and Whig

---

10. *Ibid.*, p. 159.

parties. It was during this period that the jackass representing Jackson's supposed ignorance was first used by the Whigs, only to be adopted soon after as the symbol of the Democratic party.[11]

In the election of 1828 Jackson polled 56 percent of the popular vote to win in the electoral college. His support had come in large part from the common man, the hunters of the South and northern working men. Tired of internal promotion from Cabinet to presidency, they voted for the man they felt the closest to.

Jackson began his first term of office in mourning. Rachel had died the night before the two were to leave for Washington. Unhappy and surrounded by a mediocre Cabinet, excepting Martin Van Buren, he began the task at hand. Believing the persistent lies of his supporters about the corruption of the Adams administration, Old Hickory was persuaded that his first effort must be to "cleanse the Augean stables" of accumulated filth. He shortly replaced 252 out of 612 presidential appointees, a 40 percent purge.[12] Some cases of mismanagement of funds were uncovered, but nothing compared with what would be discovered about Jackson's own appointees. Otherwise, the first two years of the Jackson administration were fairly uneventful.

Jackson had appointed an old friend from Tennessee, John Eaton, as secretary of war. He had recently married Margaret O'Neale Timberlake. This caused a great furor in Washington because Peggy Eaton had been the cause of at least one suicide and a challenge to a duel by the time she was fifteen. She had been married at sixteen, widowed at twenty-nine, and had worked as a barmaid in her father's

---

11. Samuel Eliot Morison, *The Oxford History of the American People*, p. 424.
12. *Ibid.*, p. 426.

tavern. Her reputation so outraged Washington society that no one would call on her. Jackson, standing by his old friend, urged the members of the Cabinet to call on the Eatons. Their wives refused and there was nothing the president could do. The situation was so disrupting to the functioning of the government that the secretary of state, Martin Van Buren, offered to resign. At first the general would have none of it. However, "Little Van" finally made him see that if the secretary of state resigned the balance of the Cabinet would also. John Eaton took the hint and the rest followed suit with the exception of the postmaster general. The result was that in 1830-31 Jackson was able to reconstruct his Cabinet. Edward Livingston was appointed secretary of state, Louis McLane, secretary of the Treasury, General Lewis Cass, secretary of the War Department, Levi Woodbury, secretary of the Navy, and Roger B. Taney, attorney general. With a stronger and more distinguished Cabinet behind him, Jackson determined to run for a second term.

All was not smooth, however, for the balance of the first term. In 1828 Adams had signed a new and stiffer tariff bill, later referred to as the "tariff of abominations," which created consternation both at home and abroad. This tariff, an attempt at improvement over the protective tariff legislation of 1824, which, contrary to expectations, did not alleviate financial difficulties in the South, provided for higher duties on raw materials than on manufactures. Vice-President Calhoun, leader of strong southern forces, held that any state had the right to refuse to enforce any federal law until it had been approved by three quarters of the state. Any such law, according to the nullifiers, was unconstitutional. These beliefs, fostered by the tariff laws, were most espoused by the South Carolinians. Secession, in fact, was close. After much debate over the months from January to April 1830, Jackson finally took a stand. At the Jefferson Day Dinner on April 13 the president proposed the following toast to the discouragement of the nullifiers: "Our Union: It must be preserved." It was not until January 1833 that the question was resolved. South Carolina, narrowly missing invasion by United States forces and consequent civil war, rescinded the nullification resolution. During this difficult period the Bank War was begun.

The BUS had been able to keep the economy fairly stable since the depression of 1819. This was accomplished in part by presenting notes on western banks for prompt payment in specie, thereby reducing the amount of paper credit available for speculation. These tactics, limited primarily to the western states, only served to enlarge the anti-Bank factions. As early as 1819 the BUS had been referred to as the "Monster,"[13] a term gaining popularity in the ensuing years.

However, in the East, the Bank had become a necessary part of the business mechanism. Calhoun and the Carolina nullifiers had no quarrel with it. Jackson, whose opinion was of importance because of the forthcoming recharter of the Bank (1836), shared the mistrust of his fellow westerners, but was most concerned over the development of a money power aristocracy. This, he determined, would be an enemy of democracy. He informed Nicholas Biddle, president of the Bank, "I do not dislike your bank; but since I read the history of the South Sea Bubble, I have been afraid of banks."[14] Biddle was to prove no mean adversary.

The convention of 1832, held in Baltimore and the first for the Democratic party, nominated Jackson by acclamation for a second term and approved Van Buren for the vice-

---

13. This term was first used by Thomas Hart Benton, senator from Missouri.
14. Morison, p. 438.

presidency. Jackson, though not approving of the Bank, did not make a campaign issue of it. Rather, it was Senator Clay who forced the question (and the Bank War) by bringing up the Bank recharter four years early. Not waiting until 1836 was to prove a mistake for the Bank-aligned senator, for it only roused the president's anger. Clay's recharter bill was presented to Congress and supported by Calhoun. It was passed on July 3, 1832. Jackson vetoed it. The veto, prepared with the assistance of Taney, Amos Kendall, and Jackson's nephew A. J. Donelson, was sent to the Capitol on July 10.

> Distinctions in society will always exist under every just Government. Equality of talents, of education, or of wealth, can not be produced by human institutions. In the full enjoyment of the gifts of heaven and the fruits of superior industry, economy, and virtue, every man is equally entitled to protection by law. But when the laws undertake to add to these natural and just advantages, artificial distinctions, . . . to make the rich richer and the potent more powerful, the humble members of society, the farmers, mechanics, and laborers, who have neither the time nor the means of securing like favors to themselves, have a right to complain of the injustice of their government. Its evils exist only in its abuses. If it would confine itself to equal protection, and, as heaven does its rains, shower its favors alike on the high and the low, the rich and the poor, it would be an unqualified blessing. In the act before me, there seems to be a wide and unnecessary departure from these just principles.[15]

Biddle, referring to the message as a "manifesto of anarchy," printed thirty thousand copies of it in hopes of alerting the populace to its harshness and thence turning the tide. Also, he enlisted the aid of the Bank's counsel Daniel

---

15. James, p. 303. This is a small portion of the veto presented by Jackson which describes his philosophy and fear of a money aristocracy.

Webster, who delivered his attack on the message on July 11. Webster, it should be noted, was in debt to the Bank in the sum of $22,000. The following week he was to receive an additional accommodation of $10,000. Nevertheless, on July 13 the veto was sustained by Congress. The subsequent presidential election proved an overpowering victory for Jackson. (Polling over twice as many popular votes as his nearest running mate Clay, he won 217 votes in the electoral college to Clay's 49 and Wist's 7.)

Aside from the issue of rechartering, the prospect of removing government deposits from the BUS before its dissolution in 1836 was contemplated officially in November of 1832, when the questionable conduct of the Bank in the matter of the retirement of a series of 3 percent government securities came under review. The Treasury had told Biddle that spring to be prepared to redeem six million dollars' worth of these securities on July 1. Biddle requested postponement for the reason that disbursements would disrupt commerce. In actuality, Biddle had been a little too generous in making loans to supporters of the Bank and was unable to produce the necessary funds. A "deal" was attempted with Barings, a London banking house, to buy up several millions of these securities and withhold them from the U. S. Government. The arrangement was squelched when certain information was disclosed by the press.

Jackson was furious and declared the Bank unsafe. Therefore, which would be the better course: immediate revocation of the charter or removal of government deposits? A serious investigation into the Bank's conduct was called for in his annual message to Congress. Two reports were issued: the majority report, five pages in length, pronounced the Bank sound and recommended that deposits should be retained; the minority report, eighty-four pages, gave evidence of the critical conditions of some of the western branches and of some of the questionable practices indulged in by the Bank.[16] These reports reached the House of Representatives March 1 and 2 of 1833, the last two days of that Congressional Session. Impending adjournment and the imposing length of the minority report gave Clay's supporters the opportunity to push through a resolution based on the findings of the brief majority report. On the last day of his first term of office, Jackson received the following report from the House of Representatives: "Resolved, that Government deposits may, in the opinion of the House, be safely continued in the Bank of the United States."

Jackson was not entirely wrong in his notion that the Bank was a corrupting influence. Congressmen and Senators, not to mention numerous newspapers, who supported the Bank were themselves supported handsomely. Some readily joined pro-Bank forces to ensure this end. As mentioned before, Webster was in debt to the Bank for some $32,000. He was not alone. Clayton of Georgia, Verplank of New York, Duff Green, editor of the *United States Telegraph* (Washington), were all the recipients of "loans."

Not delaying after the House passed the resolution on deposits, Jackson, on March 19, 1833, asked in a memorandum to the Cabinet the following: 1) Had anything happened since December to lessen concern for the safety of deposits? 2) Had the Bank been a faithful agent of the government? 3) Should the vetoed charter be renewed with modifications? 4) Should there be a new Bank? 5) What should be done with government revenues?[17] The answers the president received from Secretary of the Treasury McLane and Attorney General Taney were the most important. Taney, responding

---

16. *Ibid.*, p. 333.
17. *Ibid.*, p. 335.

first, began by recommending that the Bank not be re-chartered and that deposits should be removed. The alternative, he said, would be to place deposits in specially selected state banks. His arguments drew heavily on the recently uncovered and highly suspicious activities of the Bank. McLane's report came seven weeks later and consisted of ninety-one manuscript pages. He was in agreement with Taney that under no circumstances should the Bank be rechartered. However, his recommendations were that a new national bank be formed which would receive and disburse public funds. He argued that the BUS was solvent and that state banks should not be used as they were unsafe. Besides which, he said, the secretary of the Treasury was the only person who had the authority to remove deposits.

Jackson decided in favor of Taney's plan. Accordingly, that summer he sent Amos Kendall, an adviser and member of the "Kitchen Cabinet,"[18] on a visitation to the various state banks in order to determine the fitness of each to receive deposits. Before leaving for a holiday, he made two Cabinet changes: Livingston, the secretary of state, was made minister to Paris; McLane stepped into Livingston's place, and William J. Duane of Philadelphia became secretary of the Treasury.

Kendall kept in continuous contact with the president, informing him of progress made. Increasingly, banks had begun to cool toward the expectation of government deposits as Biddle began to tighten their credit in an attempt to force Jackson to give up his plans for removal of government revenues and become dependent on the BUS. During

---

18. The "Kitchen Cabinet" was a term coined to refer to Jackson's personal friends who served him in an unofficial advisory capacity, especially during his first two years in office. A few stayed on like Kendall, the only member of this group to attain Cabinet rank.

that summer and fall, Biddle placed his own bank in top condition and surreptitiously brought state banks into its debt, especially in the West and South. Loans were called in and money became scarce. The legislature of Pennsylvania, finally recognizing Biddle's intent, passed the following resolve in March 1834: "That the present bank of the United States ought not to be rechartered by congress," and "That the government deposits . . . ought not to be restored."[19] Other legislatures followed suit. In Congress the pro-Bank partisans deserted by the score. The president had won the battle and deposits flowed into state banks. Biddle, recognizing that he had lost that round, issued orders on July 11, 1834, that loosened credit and allowed the cash to flow throughout the country. In a short time, all appeared well with the economy.

Regardless of regulations, state banks could not seem to avoid speculation and more and more paper currency was produced, based only in part on government deposits. These latter, however, were nowhere near sufficient to cover the notes. Prices soared. Inflation affected all areas of the economy. A significant factor in the boom was land speculation. Government lands in the West were selling as never before and foreign speculators were investing heavily with the expectation of turning over huge profits. Payments were made for the lands with paper money, most of it from state banks, which, when presented for payment by the government, could not be redeemed in specie.

The flaws in the "pet" bank deposit system had become as obvious as the flaws in the BUS which Jackson had so long fought against. The banks were lending government funds on questionable security as well as adding quantities

---

19. James, p. 576.

of paper currency which they could not hope to redeem. Senator Benton of Missouri introduced a resolution which would allow for the purchase of government lands only with gold and silver. This, however, failed to pass Congress. The paper boom continued. As a result of the inflationary situation in which the country found itself, the president was forced to issue the famous Specie Circular—or Treasury Order, as he preferred to have it known. Presented to Congress on July 11, 1836, the Specie Circular stated essentially that paper money would no longer be accepted in payment for public lands. Prices plummeted and the land boom went bust.[20]

The Bank of the United States, lacking recharter, quietly passed from existence. Biddle, however, was not through; he formed his own bank, the United States Bank of Pennsylvania.

On March 4, 1837, Martin Van Buren became president of the United States. The "little magician," Jackson's right hand man for the past four years, had not the popularity of his predecessor. In fact, it was only because of Old Hickory's endorsement and continued efforts that he was elected at all. Entering the White House, Van Buren found himself in the midst of a financial panic. The avalanche of tumbling paper was such that it was almost impossible to stay debt free. To further distort the situation, important British business houses holding 6 percent U.S. Bonds had failed late in 1836, causing specie to flow from the U.S. and precipitating additional tightening of credit. Huge crowds led by the Locofocos, the radical wing of the Democratic party, gathered in Charlestown, Boston, and New York demanding that prices come down. In every way possible the radicals drew

---

20. Arthur M. Schlesinger, Jr., *The Age of Jackson*, p. 130-131.

attention to the plight of the workingman and the situation created by deposit banks and their "shinplasters."[21]

Concurrently, conservative Democrats, representing in large part the business and banking communities, came down hard on Van Buren in an attempt to get Jackson's Specie Circular repealed. War raged between the various factions but Van Buren stood firm and would not repeal the Circular. However, something had to be done. On May 10, 1837, the New York banks suspended specie payments, followed soon after by the rest of the banks in the country. The nationwide suspension soon brought matters to a head; not even the Conservatives could agree that the action showed a high sense of public duty. Van Buren was faced with three possibilities. He could continue support of the state banks; he could restore Biddle and the U. S. Bank or a facsimile thereof; or he could bring about a separation of bank and state by substituting an independent treasury under the government. This latter move was the only one which had not been attempted.

The idea of an independent treasury, or sub-treasury, was not a new one. It had been suggested as early as 1829 and certainly Jackson had had the option of a similar mode of action in 1833. Proponents of this plan were Thomas Hart Benton, W. M. Gouge, and Jackson waiting from his Hermitage, to name but a few. Gouge, famous for his *A Short History of Paper Money and Banking in the United States* (1833), presented Van Buren a memorandum strongly recommending the institution of the sub-treasury. This further possible extension of hard money policy created considerable

---

21. "Shinplasters," originally used as a derogatory term for fractional currency (values under $1) was later used in reference to most paper money, most of which was devalued by inflation or unredeemable in specie. Hence, they were good only for plastering one's shins.

furor throughout the summer of 1837—into the midst of which came Nicholas Biddle in an attempt to get the BUS rechartered as a deposit bank. The government was not interested.

On September 4, 1837, the president, after an analysis of the panic and the current bank situation, rejected the idea of deposit banks and recommended the independent treasury. "Locofocoism now bore the imprimatur of the White House."[22] The fighting was not over by any means but Van Buren would not yield. In 1841 the sub-treasury became a fact, continuing until the founding of the Federal Reserve in 1913.

---

22. Schlesinger, p. 235. Locofocoism, the philosophy of the radical wing of the Democratic party, represented the workingman. The movement was named after Locofocos, the newly invented friction matches, when, at an attempt by the Bank Democrats to disrupt their meeting by turning out the gas lights, the radical Democrats produced their matches, lighted candles, and continued the meeting.

THIS CARICATURE by D. C. Johnston is only one of several issued not only by Johnston but also by his contemporaries—H. R. Robinson and E. W. Clay, for example. A significant number dealt with the United States Bank and the subsequent sub-treasury proposed by Van Buren. Actual penny-sized coins or tokens were struck denouncing Jackson's and Van Buren's programs. One is even labeled "Bentonian currency—mint drop." These are known as hard times tokens.

At least two other caricature bank notes exist, though they appear cruder and less sophisticated in content. This one exists in several states. Both heavy stock paper and an onion-skin or flimsy were used, the latter being more fragile but more like the currency then in use. Also, some examples bear the imprint "Eng'd by the Locofoco shinplaster engraving Co." This cartoon was probably first issued in the fall or winter of 1837.

The title alone suggests several things. First, "Great Locofoco Juggernaut": the Locofocos, radical Democrats, are pulling the juggernaut, under which hundreds of followers are throwing themselves as sacrifices. Second, "Console-A-Tory" indicates the pressure applied by British commercial houses which was believed to be a reason behind the suggestion of the sub-treasury. Thirdly, "Sub-treasury Rag-monster" would suggest that with the formation of the sub-treasury additional worthless paper currency would flood the economy.

Van Buren himself may be seen at the top center of the engraving as a cat atop the juggernaut sitting on a bag marked "Deposits." Richard M. "Tecumseh" Johnson, Van Buren's vice-president, is probably the driver. To the right are Jackson and "John Bull" congratulating each other. In the background are burning houses and desolation, a result of the likely inefficiency of the independent treasury.

At the far right stands Jackson in the garb of an old lady. This portrayal of Old Hickory dates from the early days of his first term in office when he relied on the advice of personal friends and others outside the Cabinet. This group soon became known as the "Kitchen Cabinet." Clutched in his right hand is a staff bearing a tattered flag labeled "Constitution." In his left hand is a veto, referring to the veto of the Bank recharter in 1833. Underfoot are documents labeled "Vote of Congress," "Peoples Rights," and "Common Sense."

In the center there is the legend "Good for a Shave," with "12½ cents" and "shinplaster" in a ball. "Shinplasters" originally referred to bank notes with values under one dollar. Later, however, as currency was devalued and banks went broke or suspended payment in specie, most notes became known as shinplasters. Who it is that is setting the ball in motion is unidentified, perhaps Jackson or Benton. Below is Van Buren, ringed with a serpent labeled "Treasury Circular" (also known as the Specie Circular or Treasury Order). Under Van Buren is the name "Laocoon." (Laocoon was a Trojan priest of Apollo who, with his two sons, was killed by two serpents for warning his people of the Trojan Horse.)

Numerous puns are made on protagonists' names in the verse, as are allusions to the roles they played.

BENT-ON   Thomas Hart Benton, senator from Missouri and a long time anti-Bank leader.

WOULD-BURY   Levi Woodbury, secretary of the Treasury under Jackson.

KENN'D ALL   Amos Kendall, member of the Kitchen Cabinet and later postmaster general under Jackson.

WIT-KNEE   Reuben Whitney, a leader of the workingmen in 1829, assisted Amos Kendall in setting up the deposit system for the "pet" state banks.

VAN   Van Buren, a common nickname along with the "magician."

In addition, reference is made to the bank of Mississippi, the only bank to continue payments in specie during the panics of the 1820s and 30s. The cartoon is signed "Loco Foco" and countersigned "Accepted—Ben Ton," Thomas Hart Benton again.

To the left is a jackass with the head of Jackson. Following rather too closely behind the ass, hat in hand as if waiting for a handout, may be seen Van Buren with the body of a monkey. Below is the caption "Treading in the footsteps of his illustrious & c." The signpost points "To Ruin."

Behind Van Buren is a vignette showing a hand holding a bag of gold. The caption reads "YELLOW BOYS—OFFICE HOLDERS PAY." In front of Jackson is a similar vignette of a hand holding paper money labeled "Good for a Shave." Here the caption reads "TREASURY RAGS—PEOPLES PAY."

Reflected in Johnston's satire on the sub-treasury are many of the predominant attitudes held by businessmen and bankers of the 1830s, as well as those of conservative political persuasion. First, that Van Buren, the "little magician," was following Jackson's dictates and the pressure from British banking and commercial interests. Second, that the workingmen whose plight was to be averted by the sub-treasury would instead be crushed by the new "monster," and those who would benefit would be officials and the moneyed aristocracy. Third, that the new sub-treasury would produce "rags" or "shinplasters" as worthless as the worst of the bank notes to date. And finally, that the sub-treasury was a ploy to gain votes and advance the political aspirations of certain office holders. Whether these were Johnston's personal views or not is not known. However, it is reasonable to assume from his other satires that he expressed no love for Andrew Jackson and his policies, and that he may well have shared the beliefs pictured herein.

Bibliography and Suggested Reading.

Boston Monthly Magazine, "Lithography," Vol. I, No. VI, Boston, December, 1825.

Brigham, Clarence F., *David Claypoole Johnston, The American Cruikshank*. Proceedings of the American Antiquarian Society, Davis Press, Worcester, Mass. 1940.

(Davis, Charles A.) *Letters of J. Downing, Major*. Harper and Brothers, New York, 1834.*

Dunlap, William, *History of the Rise and Progress of the Arts of Design in the United States*. Benjamin Blom, New York, 1965.

Gouge, W. M., *A Short History of Paper Money and Banking in the United States*, Philadelphia, 1833.

Hamilton, Sinclair, *Early American Book Illustrators and Wood Engravers, 1670-1870*. Princeton University Press, Princeton, 1968.

James, Marquis, *The Wife of Andrew Jackson*, The Bobbs-Merrill Company, New York, 1937.

Johnson, Malcolm, *David Claypool Johnston, American Graphic Humorist, 1798-1865*. A catalog for an exhibition held jointly at The American Antiquarian Society, Boston College, The Boston Public Library, and The Worcester Art Museum, March, 1970.

Morison, Samuel Eliot, *The Oxford History of the American People*. Oxford University Press, New York, 1965.

Murrell, Wilham, *A History of American Graphic Humor*. Vol. I, Whitney Museum of American Art, New York, 1938.

Schlesinger, Arthur M., Jr., *The Age of Jackson*. Little, Brown, and Company, Boston, 1953.

Smith, Seba, *The Wife and Writings of Major Jack Downing*, Lilly, Wait, Colman, and Holden, Boston, 1833. (Illustrated by D. C. Johnston.)*

---

* Both of these are humorous commentaries on the Jackson Administration.

[35]

Tatham, David, "A Note About David Claypoole Johnston." *The Courier*, No. 34, pp. 11-17, Syracuse University Library Associates, 1970.

Tatham, David, "A Check List of David Claypoole Johnston's Book Illustrations." *The Courier*, No. 35, pp. 26-31, Syracuse University Library Associates, 1970.

Van Deusen, Glydden, *The Jacksonian Era, Eighteen Twenty Eight to Eighteen Forty Eight*. Harper & Row, New York, 1959.

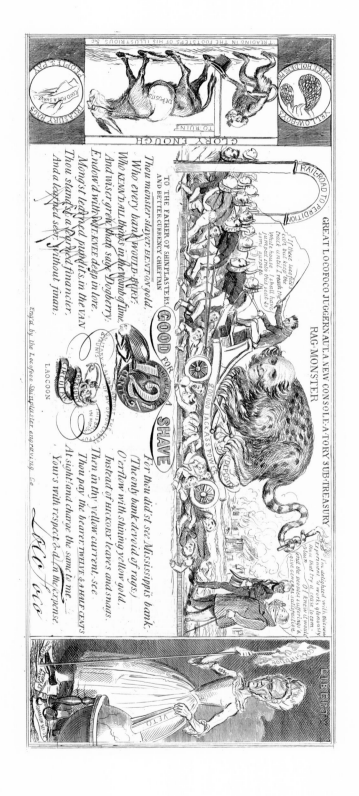

THIS KEEPSAKE VOLUME was designed by Bert Clarke and composed and printed under his supervision at the Press of A. Colish in Mount Vernon, New York. The text type is Monotype Fournier. The D. C. Johnston cartoon, which is laid in, was restruck from the original engraved copperplate belonging to the American Antiquarian Society by Woodbury & Company, both of Worcester, Massachusetts. The line engravings in the text are reproduced from Johnston's etchings for his *Scraps No. 7 for the Year 1837*, an issue parodying phrenology. On page fourteen is a self-portrait, on page thirty Johnston's office front at 6 Summer Street, Boston, while the cartoon above spoofs the phrenological trait of watchfulness. The illustrations on the cover and title page were made from a copper "hard times" token struck in 1837 as a satirical comment on Van Buren and the sub-treasury. The paper is Mohawk Superfine Text. The binding is by Publishers Book Bindery in Long Island City, New York.

Of 1950 copies printed, this is number .